War? I'm Scared!

WeWrite Kids!™ Book #46

*Written by
WeWrite Kids*

**Tim Beadle
Katie Edwards
Tera Edwards
Emily Goetsch
Taylor Harmon
Chelsea Hermes
Lance Morgan
Zac Stephens**

Story illustrations by Norman E. Calmese

Graphic design by E-motion

We Write
BOOKS BY KIDS - FOR KIDS!
Rochester, Illinois

BOOKS BY KIDS - FOR KIDS!

For information regarding:
WeWrite Kids!™ Books,
WeWrite Book-Writing Workshops,
and products contact:

WeWrite Corporation
300 Pakey Road
Springfield, Illinois 62707

Mailing address:
P.O. Box 498
Rochester, Illinois 62563
(217) 498-8458 • 1-800-295-9037
FAX (217) 498-7524
www.wewrite.net • email: info@wewrite.net

War? I'm Scared!
ISBN 1-57635-057-6 (Softcover) $8.95
WeWrite Kids!™ Book #46
By WeWrite Kids
Story illustrations by Norman E. Calmese
Cover & graphics by E-motion

Credits:
Cover and story illustrations: **Norman E. Calmese**
Book design, layout, and color: **E-motion**,
www.emotionusa.com
Photos: **Robert Andrews**
Senior editor: **Jacqueline Goodwin**
Assistant editors: **Sarah Schuppan, Suzanne Fisher**
Book printing and binding:
Multi-Ad Services, Inc., Peoria, Illinois
www.multi-ad.com

Foreword

"Where were you on the morning of September 11, 2001?" That is a question most of us can answer. For many individuals in the United States of America, the answer is, "In my grade school classroom." And that is the answer for the authors of this book. After that morning, these young people, like so many others, found themselves dealing with the fear of terrorism and with life and death...probably for the first time.

As the 2001 Illinois Mother of the Year, the responses of children throughout the nation are important to me.

In the creation of *War? I'm Scared!*, the young writers have been able to capture the essence of the fear experienced by so many. They have given a healthy illustration of how to handle that fear. After all, if brave and loving dogs like Buddy and Nikki can make a positive difference in the face of a national disaster, surely young people can too!

The attack on the World Trade Center buildings was obviously beyond the control of the young citizens who have written this book. They have reminded us, however, that our response to that tragedy is completely within our control. *War? I'm Scared!* encourages every reader, young and old, to choose to respond to the victims of disaster in a caring and compassionate way...and to realize that EVERYONE can positively affect our world.

By Kendra Smiley, 2001 Illinois Mother of the Year
Popular national speaker, author of several books, including Helping Your Kids Make Good Choices, wife of United States Air Force Reserve Pilot, Colonel John Smiley
www.kendrasmiley.com

I'm Stixx. I run all over the words in the story. While you read, write down the letters I'm touching. It will spell out a secret message.

Answer: page 59

Cars whiz by. There are lots of cars in New York City. If I could just catch one, I'd be the fastest Golden Retriever ever. Look! There's a police car. My favorite! I like the shiny, flashing lights. My paws reach out in front of me. I'm SuperBuddy. My legs spin like crazy. Almost got it....

Sniff. Ham? Sniff...sniff. Mmmmmm. Ham. Snurf-f-f-f. And pancakes. Eating ham and pancakes is even better than chasing cars! I turn to follow the yummy smell.

Jingle. Jingle. My clinking dog tags wake me up. Opening my eyes, I yawn and look around.

Huh? No police car? No ham and pancakes? It was just a dream? Awww…. But it's OK. I'm here in my soft, cozy bed.

I look over at my owner. She's still sleeping. Her curly, brown hair is spread all over her pillow. Her name is Shelley. Sigh.

Happily, I roll over and stretch.

Wait! I sit up quickly. Sniff. Ham and pancakes! The smell is warm and sweet. Snif-f-f-f-f-f. My stomach gurgles and growls. Maybe it's coming from the pancake parlor next door. Sometimes the nice people give me food they are throwing out. They like me. I'm polite and always do the tricks they ask me to do. "Buddy, sit up." "Roll over." "Play dead, Boy." I know them all.

My stomach grumbles again. I'm so hungry. Jumping out of my basket, I walk over to Shelley. She's snoring. I push her hand up with my nose, hoping to wake her up. But her hand just flops. She must be really tired. How will I get breakfast now?

Just then, a breeze blows the curtains back toward the bed. The window is open! I'll go get breakfast by myself. Yeah, that's what I'll do. I put my front paws on the windowsill and stick my head outside.

Mmmm, the ham-and-pancake smell again. Closing my eyes, I follow the smell and let my nose lead me out of Shelley's room and on to the fire escape. Smack, smack, smack. Licking my lips, I head toward the ladder.

Oh no! The ladder is pulled up! Now what? I look over the ledge and see a dumpster within jumping distance. We are only on the second floor. I can make it if I just push off really hard….

Ooompf! Thuddity-thud! I hit the dumpster lid and tumble into a pile of boxes. Ooohhhh, my head! Slowly, I try to sit up. Everything is spinning and looks weird.

I look up to see if Shelley heard the noise. Her head doesn't peek out of the window. Good, I made it.

Still dizzy, I climb out of the boxes and wobble down the alley toward the sidewalk.

Walking slowly, I turn the corner and rest on the stairs in front of my apartment building. My eyes try to focus on the blurry street. There are a lot more cars today. Two of everything. Oh! My head hurts.

Two police cars with flashing lights and sirens race by. My favorite thing to chase!

Running after the police cars, I forget all about my hurting head and the ham and pancakes.

Just then, a cat runs past and jumps on top of a bright red car that is parking in front of me. Growling, I leap after it and land on the hood.

Hon-n-n-k-k! The car horn blasts in my ears as I slide backward, tumbling onto the sidewalk. Ker - plop! The cat runs off and the car begins to drive away.

Owwww! My ears hurt. And that cat got away. Bark! Bark! Bark! I yell at the car, even though I'm not supposed to bark in our neighborhood.

BOOM! KA-BANG! The air shakes with the noise. What was that? Did I do that? Scared, I put my tail between my legs and run back to my apartment building. Oh no! I shouldn't have barked so loud!

I hear Shelley. "Buddy! Buddy, come here!"

Uh oh, I can tell by Shelley's voice that something is wrong. I'm in big trouble now. I bet I have to go into my cage.

I slink past her into the living room. I wait. And wait.

After what seems like forever, I look up. Shelley isn't looking at me. She's looking out the window with her eyes and mouth wide open. I look, too, and see a big, black ball of smoke and fire coming from the top of the World Trade Center.

Boy, I'm in for it now. First, I snuck out of our apartment. Then I barked and made something explode. Now there are fires. I should have followed the rules. Whimper…whimper.

People are running outside. I hear screaming and honking. Shelley doesn't move.

Ohhhhh. I am going to be sent to that dog prison my friends told me about. They make you use CAT litter when you go to the

bathroom. You have to meow instead of bark. And worst of all, they make you eat CAT food mixed with CABBAGE. Yuck!

I hear more people running and screaming. Sirens. They're coming to get me. I
have to hide. The couch! I'll hide behind the
couch. Un-n-h-h. I squeeze in behind it.
Scared and shaking, I put my paws over my

head and close my eyes tight. I try to be very
small. No one will find me now.

Whimper. I feel really bad. Shelley is
mad at me. I broke things. And now they are
going to take me to prison. Ohhhhh!

Shelley stops being frozen and turns

away from the window. She hears me behind the couch and sees me shaking and
scared. Kneeling down, she pets me gently.

"It's OK, Buddy, it's going to be OK."

Why isn't she mad? Maybe she doesn't
know it was me. I don't understand. She
talks to me calmly and hugs me. I start to
feel a little better.

"Let's turn on the news and see what's

going on. Come on. Everything will be all right." Shelley's voice is shaking.

I put my head on her lap. She scratches my ears and plays with my chain collar in her loving way. I want to believe her.

The TV person says an airplane hit the World Trade Center. What? I snap my head up and watch the pictures showing the building I thought I broke.

It wasn't me? I didn't do it? Really? Whew! I feel so relieved. Butterflies feel like they are flying out of my stomach. I can hardly sit still. I wag my tail faster and faster with happiness.

But something is still wrong.

Shelley doesn't take her eyes off the TV. Her hand holds on tightly to my fur. Another orange and black ball of fire is shown on the news. It's right next to the other building on fire. Shelley picks up the phone and dials a number.

"Hello, Mom? I know…I know…I'm watching it, too. Yes, I'm fine. I just wanted

to let you know that Buddy and I are going to the church until it is safe for us to come back home. That's part of our disaster plan.

Will you meet me there? Good. See you soon."

What is she doing? I feel nervous when she puts things into a suitcase. Shelley mutters as she reads our WHAT TO DO IN AN EMERGENCY list out loud.

"Just stay calm." she breathes.

She packs some of my dog food, my bowls, and my bed. Good, she remembers my bed. I love my bed.

Shelley hurries around, making sure everything is turned off before we leave. After the apartment is taken care of, she whistles for me to follow her.

As Shelley locks the apartment door, a fireman and his Dalmatian run up the stairs.

"Hello Ma'am. My name is Dave. Good, I see you're leaving. We're evacuating this building and checking to make sure all the gas lines and electrical wires are all right. We'll be turning off the water, gas, and power for now."

Shelley nods at Dave. "We were just going to the church. That's where the emergency shelter is for this area."

"Great. You're doing the right thing."

While the fireman asks Shelley some

questions, the Dalmatian walks over to me, wagging his tail.

"Hi. My name is Oreo. I work with Fireman Dave," he says proudly. "We're making sure everyone leaves their apartments so that they will be safe. What's your name?"

"Buddy." I say, impressed that a dog is helping.

"Buddy. Like 'Good Buddy?'"

"Yeah." Buddy smiles.

Oreo continues, "Just stay with your owner and go to a safe place." Oreo nods wisely at me and then leads Fireman Dave up the stairs.

Shelley carries our things downstairs. Following close behind, I think about Oreo and his important job.

When we get outside, we see more

people leaving with bags. They're crying and some people are screaming. I hear more sirens and feel afraid again.

"Come on, Buddy. Let's go." Shelley pats the back seat.

My feet won't move. I've never seen anything this scary. She calls me again, this time louder, but I just stay.

She groans, "Oh Buddy. Please, not now." Stomping her feet, Shelley comes over and picks me up. "Come on, Buddy! We have to get moving!"

Pushing me into in the back seat, she closes the door. I feel trapped.

Shelley gets into the driver's seat and jams the car in between two trucks in the road. There are so many cars that they are hardly moving. People are yelling and look-ing at the black clouds swirling around the two buildings. H-o-n-n-n-k-k-k! Traffic is moving an inch a minute. Shelley suddenly takes a deep breath, then whispers, "Ohhhh noooo!" I look out and see one building

crumble down into a huge, smoky, gray cloud.

I start whining and whimpering. What is going on? I just want to go home and curl up in my bed. Why won't all of this scary stuff stop? Scratching at the window and door, I try to get out.

"Settle down, Buddy. It's going to be OK."

Crawling onto the floor behind Shelley's seat, I hide my eyes. Suddenly Shelley gasps. I lift my head up to look out the window. The second building comes down in a big cloud of dust. Whi-i-i-i-n-n-e.

Shelley tells me to calm down again, as she turns on the radio. The people talking sound very serious. They say what happened today is an Act of War.

War? I'm scared!

"Oh no, this is awful!" Shelly moans.

I keep staring at the smoke and dust in the sky.

"Don't worry, Buddy, we are going to a safer place." She tries to talk to me calmly.

I keep looking out the window, watching everything happening in the city. At least I am here, with Shelley. I guess this is the best place to be right now.

On the way to the church, we keep getting stuck in traffic. We get stopped on the street that leads to the World Trade Center. I

see people with jackets putting people carefully into ambulances. Firefighters are spraying water on the fires. Some police officers are keeping people back from entering the dangerous area. Ahead, there is a Great Dane sitting next to a police officer directing traffic. Shelley stops.

"Excuse me, can you tell me if I can get to the church shelter this way?"

The policewoman shakes her head. "No, you are going to have to turn around and take a different street."

While she gives Shelley directions, I stick my nose outside Shelley's window to talk to the dog. She doesn't look scared.

Trying to keep my voice from shaking, I ask, "Hey, I'm Buddy. What are you doing here?"

The Great Dane only turns her head toward me. "I'm Officer Savannah--a police dog. And I'm working." Officer Savannah looks down the street at the World Trade Center. "I'm helping to keep people away from those burning buildings. People are trying to get a closer look at what happened. It's too dangerous. We also need to keep them away so that the firemen can get in there. We'll be going to help search, too."

I look at the buildings, the smoke, the people, and feel nervous. "Aren't you scared?"

Officer Savannah straightens up. "Sure, but this is my job. It makes me feel good to rescue people. We search-and-rescue dogs can fit into little spaces better than people. That means we can look for those who are hurt in areas the rescue workers can't reach."

Shelley thanks the officer for the directions and we drive away. I want to help, too. But how?

The cars move so slowly, it seems like we are in the car forever. I am glad when we finally get to the church. A lot of people are there. Inside, everyone is crying and praying. A church leader and some helpers are handing out blankets and pillows. Some beds are set up in the aisles. Everyone is talking about what happened.

Shelley finds an open bed and sits down on it, exhausted. She puts my bed on the floor next to her. Ah, my bed. I get on it, but can't even think about sleep now.

"Mom! Dad!" Shelley jumps up, runs over to the door, and hugs her parents. I'm excited because Nikki is with them. Nikki is a Cocker Spaniel—we're best friends. Shelley's parents live in New York, too, and we get to see them all the time.

Nikki runs up to me, wagging her tail. "Hi Buddy! Are you OK?"

I wag my tail back. "Yeah. But I'm kind of scared. Everything's so confusing. I'm glad we're all here together. I feel a lot safer."

Nikki agrees. "Me, too. Maybe we can walk around and see what everyone is doing."

Shelley talks quietly with Mom. Dad goes to help a worker greet more people at the door. More and more people come to the church. Someone brings in some boxes of food and they begin to pass out sand- wiches.

Some kids share their sandwiches with us. Nikki says, "Hey, this is all right."

One man is looking out the window

with a pair of binoculars and telling two women what he sees. People are listening to radios. There's a television turned on in the front of the church. A nursery area is in the corner, with a group of kids playing a game there. The news is on, but the kids aren't listening.

"I don't want to watch the news, either," I tell Nikki. "They're talking about war and it's too scary." She nods her head and we wander back to our area.

Suddenly, Shelley jumps up. "Andrew! What are you doing here?" She runs over and gives him a hug. "Mom, Dad, this is my friend, Andrew. He is an officer in the Navy."

Andrew steps forward and shakes their hands. "Nice to meet you. This is my dog, Lightning. He's in the Navy, too." Andrew gives the German Shepherd a hand signal, telling him that he can relax.

Lightning comes over and sits by us while Andrew talks to Shelley. Nikki looks at him, interested.

"I'm Buddy and this is Nikki. You're a Navy dog, huh? Lightning... Great name. You must be fast."

Lightning smiles. "Yes sir! Are you and your family all right?"

I nod my head. "Yes, we came down here right after it happened. Firemen came and made everyone leave our apartment building. What do you do in the Navy?"

Lightning tells us proudly, "We make sure people are safe. Andrew and I are going down to the site to look for people who need help. We came here first to see if anyone needs anything."

We all stop talking and listen to Andrew. He is explaining what is happening to a group of worried people. No one says a word as they listen.

"It looks like those airplanes hit important places on purpose. We don't understand what happened or why or who yet. Not only were the World Trade Center buildings hit, but the Pentagon, too. The Pentagon is a huge building where people who protect the United States work. We think many people were hurt in these attacks. Rescue workers are there now."

Questions swarm around Andrew, until he puts his hand up for silence.

"I know there are many questions. But we don't have answers yet. You can all help by staying here so rescuers can move around quickly. We've also set up a blood donation station, for those who want to donate blood. I know many of you are looking for family and friends who work in or around the World Trade Center." Andrew points to a message board. "There's a list of numbers you can call for more information. Please keep everyone in your prayers." He hurries off, calling Lightning with a hand signal.

"Lightning, come."

Lightning answers Andrew with a bark and then turns to us. "Take care, Buddy and Nikki. Maybe I'll see you again."

Nikki and I look at each other as Lightning runs to Andrew's side, ready for action. We are both thinking the same thing.

I say to Nikki, "We have to do something, too. How can we help?"

We both look around the room, trying to think of ideas.

"Well," Nikki says, with her eyes brightening, "we can keep people company. They can pet us. That always makes my family feel better when they feel bad."

"Great idea!" I bark excitedly. "And we can play with the kids so they won't be scared by what's on the news."

Looking around, I go over to a little girl who is watching TV. She looks scared. Nikki picks a ball up and drops it at her feet, but the girl just sits there. Nikki pushes the ball with her nose and races after it, bringing it to the little girl. The little girl rolls it this time and they both race after it. Soon the little girl is laughing. They play the game over and over. Nikki can't stop wagging her tail.

I find an older man who is crying and gently stick my nose under his arm. He stops crying and pets me. Playing with my dog tags, I see a smile spread across his face.

"Buddy?" He says as I lick his hand. "I had a dog like you and he was my buddy, too."

Looking for Nikki, I notice that other

kids are playing with her, too. Even grown-ups are watching, their faces in smiles. Yes! This is how we can help!

During the next few days, Nikki and I keep doing our "jobs." It is really working. When we see people crying, we snuggle up next to them so they can hug us. Shelley and her Mom tell people about what we are doing. They say, "Hugs always make a person feel better and animals have a special something."

We play with the children in the nursery area. I even give piggyback rides to the smaller kids. We notice a change all over the shelter.

Everyone helps each other more. Parents read their children stories, instead of just having them watch TV. I like listening to the sound of voices reading, too.

Shelley tells funny puppy stories about me as she passes out sandwiches and bottled water. Mom and Dad do lots of hugging, comforting, and helping. Even though everyone is scared and worried, we all make new friends. It's as though we are a giant, friendly family.

Finally, on the fourth day after the buildings fell, I hear on a radio that it is OK to go back to our homes. Yahoo! I run to find Nikki. She is playing with a girl named Lilly. They're rolling a ball back and forth to each other. Lilly laughs and claps her hands each time Nikki pushes the ball with her nose. Lilly is no longer scared and crying, like when she arrived.

"We can go back to our homes now." I bark at Nikki excitedly, jumping around.

I tell Nikki what the man on the radio said. With a final roll of the ball and a lick on the cheek for Lilly, we run as fast as we can back to our owners.

Shelley kneels down and hugs me around my neck. "Well Buddy, I guess we can go home now. You and Nikki are such

good dogs. You've made so many people happier just by doing what you do best— loving. Let's go say goodbye and good luck to all our new friends."

Everyone in the church is busy. Some get their things together. Others help to put the beds, blankets, and pillows away. Suddenly, I hear someone say, "Shhhhhhh!" A man in front of the church turns the television up. The TV screen shows the American flag with military people standing at attention. The National Anthem is being played.

All the people in the shelter stand and put their hands on their hearts and sing. They are loud and it sounds beautiful. Nikki and I look around and listen, wishing we could sing the words, too.

I raise my nose into the air and howl. Ahhhwoooooo! Nikki does the same. No one stops singing even though we see tears and smiles as they watch us adding our voices. After the song, people stand still, like in a spell. Shelley, Mom, and Dad hug us for a long time, wetting our fur with tears.

After a few minutes, Dad asks, "Shelley, do you want us to go back to your apartment? We can stay a few days."

Relieved, Shelley says, "Yes! Thanks! Nikki can ride back with us."

She's glad her parents will be there. I'm glad because Nikki will be there, too.

On the way back to our apartment, Nikki and I stare out the window and look at the city. A lot of smoke is still in the air. We pass by a hospital where people are lined up to give blood. We see people unloading boxes full of cans from a truck. I look where the World Trade Center used to be.

A smoking, gray mountain of broken pieces of building is in its place. People in metal hats, firehats, and heavy coats climb all over, searching. We see dogs climbing the mountain, too. They go into holes, come out, and go into another hole as fast as they can. Nikki and I know they are looking for people who are hurt. I look for Lightning and Savannah.

When we get back to our apartment, I am surprised by all the gray ash covering our building. I'm worried our building has burned, too. But when we get inside, we see everything is still OK.

"The lights and gas are back on," Shelley says.

As Nikki and I race happily around the place, Mom and Shelley start to make supper. Suddenly, someone knocks on the door. Shelley sounds surprised when she sees who it is.

"Andrew!"

Andrew comes in with Lightning. They are both covered with gray dust. Looking very tired, they drag themselves into the living room. "I just wanted to come by and see if we can stay here for the night. Lightning and I have been working at the site and we are tired, hungry, and dirty. Your apartment is much closer than ours. I thought maybe we could just sleep here, if it's OK."

"Of course." Shelly says and gives Andrew a big hug. "You and Lightning are welcome. Come on, go wash up. You can eat, then sleep on the couch."

Shelley leads Andrew to the bathroom while Nikki and I gather around Lightning.

"Lightning? You look awful! We looked for you when we passed the World Trade Center. Were you there?"

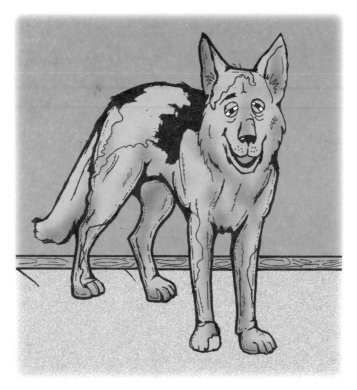

Lightning nods his head, tiredly. "I am worn out. Andrew and I were helping people for the last three days. We helped the firemen, too. It's really dangerous there. Lots of smoke and ash is in the air and it hurts when you breathe or get it in your eyes. Sometimes I stepped on sharp, hot things and cut my feet." He lifted up his front paw to show us his burned and cut foot.

Then his tired eyes brightened. "We helped save a fireman today! Everyone was yelling with happiness when I found him. And he talked to us! That was exciting. They took him to the hospital and said he's going to be OK."

Nikki and I look at each other. "Can we help too, Lightning?"

Lightning yawns. "People are finding lots of ways to help. Some donate blood. Some bring clothes and eyewash. Others bring food and water. It's amazing how we're all like a huge team." Lightning licks his hurting paw. "But we heard of some real heroes when we were down at the station. I heard them talking about a couple of dogs working downtown at a church shelter. And the dogs weren't even police, fire, or military dogs, either. People said that those dogs were turning scared and worried strangers into happier, helpful friends. You wouldn't happen to know who they were, would you?" Lightning asks with a knowing look.

Nikki and I nudge each other. Suddenly I get an idea. "I know Shelley, Mom, and Dad are going down to donate blood and help out at the shelter. We can bring our dog food down there for all the rescue dogs."

Lightning nods, yawning. "It's great that so many people and dogs are coming together. Everyone really cares." Lightning yawns again. "I'm beat." His legs fold under him. He's asleep even before his head settles

on his paws.

Nikki and I snuggle up next to him. I fall asleep thinking. "Tomorrow we will get back to work, doing what we do best-giving love. Even though we're little, we can still make a difference."

The WeWrite Kids

Front row, (left to right)
**Zac Stephens, Lance Morgan,
Emily Goetsch.**

Back row, (left to right)
**Tera Edwards, Taylor Harmon,
Katie Edwards, Tim Beadle,
Chelsea Hermes.**

Brainstorming, the kids add fresh
ideas. As the story unfolds, it's hard
to contain their excitement.

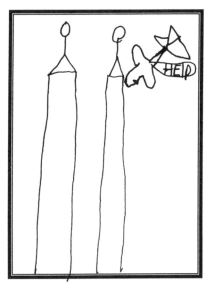

**Tim Beadle
Age 8**
"The Trade Center
falling makes me feel
sad for other people."

By Tim Beadle

**Katie Edwards
Age 10**
"I think the President
is making a decision
about having a war or
not. God is always
with you."

By Katie Edwards

Tera Edwards
Age 10

"The best part is the excitement, feelings, and action. I get to think and write out what's on my mind."

By _Tera Edwards_

Emily Goetsch
Age 10

"I liked drawing this and making up your own drawings and stories. I feel bad that our world is in danger."

By _Emily Goetsch_

Taylor Harmon
Age 9 ½

"The dog is funny. We made him funny. It's weird that I'm helping write a book."

By _Taylor Harmon_

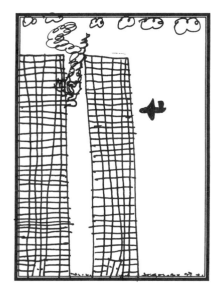

By _Chelsea Hermes_

Chelsea Hermes
Age 10

"It was fun. My favorite part was thinking about what the dog's going to do and hearing other people's ideas. I feel bad about what happened in New York. I wish it never happened. Hopefully, God will keep us safe. I don't think God wants it to happen again."

Lance Morgan
Age 11

"I like saying the stuff from my point of view. It's a kid's book for schools and stuff. Instead of reading gory stuff they can read this and get facts off this book."

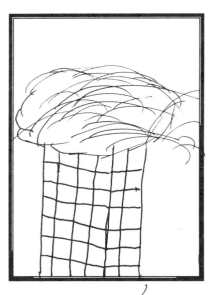

By *Lance Morgan*

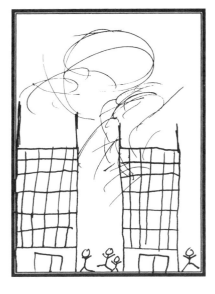

Zac Stephens
Age 11

"I like making up stuff about the story. And because it's made up from the kids' point of view."

By *Zac stephens*

49

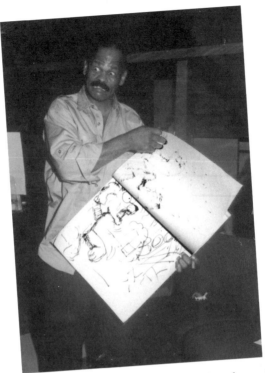

Artist Norman Calmese shares his sketches with the children and acts out Buddy's feelings.

NORMAN E. CALMESE

The idea of this project found its birthplace in the creative mind of artist Norman E. Calmese, Founder of Calmese Cartoon Factory. He believes that children's perspectives of the events of September 11, 2001 are important. WeWrite Corporation and Calmese Cartoon Factory join in bringing children's views about the war to the world.

Calmese, a native of Chicago, Illinois, lives in Springfield, Illinois. He has a Master's Degree in Community Arts Management from University of Illinois at Springfield. He also has a Bachelor of Arts Degree in Sociology and an Associate of Arts Degree in Art and History from Northern Illinois University.

As an entrepreneur, Calmese has designed cartoon logos and promotional materials for major corporations. He has over 25 years of experience in corporate America.

Calmese is publicly known as an illustrator, cartoonist, sculptor, and muralist. He has published works and illustrations in over eleven books. Calmese cartoons have appeared in *The Chicago Sun-Times, Michigan Chronicles, The Daily Defender, Wisconsin Courier,* as well as other newspapers. Honorable mentions include his collage creation for a Chicago Museum of Science and Industry publication.

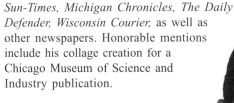

Calmese is known for spearheading mural projects in the Springfield area, which include schools, buildings, and offices. Collaborating with WeWrite Corporation, he designed and illustrated *Springfield, Illinois: A Cool Place To Be* coloring book. Illustrations for *WHINE OUT*, another WeWrite Kids!™ book are among his many accomplishments.

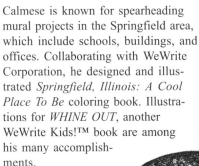

Deeply religious, Calmese believes that everyone has God-given artistic talents and the opportunity to express it. It is up to each person to explore, develop, and implement the "power of creativity" to perfect it.

Perspectives

From a teacher:
As President Bush has said, "It was not only four planes that were hijacked on September 11, 2001, but so was the Islamic faith." We must be careful not to blame all Muslims for what were the acts of only a few horribly misguided individuals.

America's six million Muslims are making notable contributions in the areas of business, economics, science, medicine, architecture, education, and many other fields. They see their religion as not only a belief system, but also as a way of life. It governs what they eat; how they interact with others; the way in which they treat their parents; the emphasis they place on education; and the development of a strong social consciousness.

Islam focuses on helping individuals to develop a highly personal relationship with God. This is accomplished in part through an individual's declaration of faith, offering a minimum of five obligatory daily prayers, fasting from dawn to sunset during the month of Ramadan, alms giving, and the pilgrimage to the city of Mecca at least once in a lifetime.

The number of Muslims living in America is growing daily. Islam is now the second largest and fastest growing religion in America. By learning more, we will be better equipped to build bridges of understanding between individuals of all faiths and backgrounds.

To learn more, contact the Council on America-Islamic Relations (CAIR) by phone at (202) 488-8787 or visit their website at www.cair-net.org.

Leila M. Mostoufi, Elementary School Teacher, Springfield, Illinois

From a crisis counselor:
Listen closely to the questions children ask.

Answer only questions that they ask. Giving too much information before they are ready won't be helpful.

Show children where the World Trade Center was and where Afghanistan is in relation to their own home. Understanding where the war is going on helps children feel comforted.

Sometimes children who are troubled about their safety and don't talk about it will have nightmares.

Talking about the nightmares the next morning is important.

Remember that dreams are more symbolic than real.

Gene Brodland, L.C.S.W. *has spent nearly forty years as a family therapist. He is in private practice with Bohlen & Associates in Springfield, Illinois. He counsels parents on how to be more effective parents and encourages children to read as a way to improve their minds. Brodland tells parents that reading is the best way to stretch thinking abilities and increase creative skills.*

From an airport director:
Talk to your child before a flight to let them know what to expect regarding their behavior.

Sound positive and excited to reduce any fears they may have.

Instruct them on the seriousness of the security screening process.

Do not let them carry on such things as scissors or other sharp items.

Children do best on short flights, early in the day. Keep your child in his seat (with seat belt on) at all times except to visit the bathroom facility.

Bring along books, games, and snacks to entertain children on long flights.

Take the opportunity to view the landscape from a bird's eye view out of an airplane window. Let them experience the wonders of seeing the clouds and possible landmarks below. (Bring an atlas to identify locations below.)

If your child is fearful of flying, let him sit in the aisle seat where he may be more comfortable, rather than looking out the window.

Do not let your child fly with an earache or cold. The change in air pressure may be painful.

Make sure small children drink plenty of water.

Take along a stomach remedy to relieve any stomach discomfort during flight.

Bob O'Brien, Jr. A.A.E., Executive Director of Aviation, Capital Airport, Springfield, Illinois. www.flyspi.com

From the military:
If called upon, we in the military understand that we may have to put ourselves in harm's way. We've accepted that this is our obligation, as military personnel. It's why we're in the military–to protect the people of our country. Trust in the government and military that we are doing the right thing.

Captain Bruce Schempp, Detachment Commander, 687th Quartermaster Battalion, Decatur, Illinois, U.S. Army Federal Reserves

Stixx's Secret Message:

Stand together.